WORDS OF WISDOM

WORDS OF WISDOM

MARGARET BROWN

Wasteland Press

Shelbyville, KY USA
www.wastelandpress.net

Words of Wisdom
By Margaret Brown

Printed in the U.S.A.

ACKNOWLEDGEMENT

I want to thank God for blessing me with this gift. I want to give thanks to my mother Nancy who is my biggest critic and cheerleader. She's always praising me for all my endeavors and this book is no exception. I want to give love to my family for always being supportive. I want my daughter Jamila to know that mommy will always be okay. I know she understands my vision. I want to give a special thanks to my brother Tzar for knowing and loving me always. I don't want to forget my friends for respecting my time and space for me to finish my projects. I want to thank my brother Junior for encouraging me to finish my current projects. Last but not least, I want to give a special thanks to Antonio for designing the cover for EXPRESSIONS OF A STRONG WILLED WOMAN.

EXCERPT

I have many stories to tell,
They were a burden that made my thoughts
swell,

Releasing the context from my mind,
Put me in a better place to unwind,

At times I'd be angry and couldn't understand,
How could I feel better with just a pen in my
hand?

I was contemplating writing a book,
There were many topics I had to take a second
look,

Should I consider a love story?
Too many in circulation I might as well do a
science fiction that's gory,

I'm leaning towards a suspense thriller,
Maybe about a cold blooded killer,

Looking over my bookshelf there's a selective
mix,
I should start soon to find that perfect fix.

TABLE OF CONTENTS

31. Feel Free
32. Food
33. Forever Young
34. Forward March
35. Greed
36. Gone
37. Grief
38. How Deep
39. Imagination
40. I'm Too Much for You
41. I Want
42. Kindness
43. Lay it Down
44. Learning
45. May I Suggest
46. Me
47. No Doubts
48. Once
49. Nobody Ask Me to Dance Anymore
50. Our World
51. Personal Journey
52. Personalities
53. Possibilities
54. Power
55. Reality
56. Restructure
57. Role Model
58. Rotten
59. Rush
60. Same Gender
61. Secret
62. Self

ACCOUNTABILITY

If you expect goodness look inward bound,
You're mad with yourself there's no need to look
around,

If you choose the wrong person in your life,
You made that mistake for becoming the wife,

If happiness is what you are in search to find,
Put your own energy in it and preserve your
time,

If you're carrying the world like a boulder,
Don't dump your hate on someone else's
shoulder,

If your always late and talking trash,
Expecting other people to love you stop before
you crash,

Pretending to fool others is a tricky antidote,
You better learn to cope.

DON'T

Don't deny who you are,

Because you shine like a star,

Don't deny who you've become,

 Belittling your greatness makes you seem dumb,

Don't deny your fire,

That's self loathing and defeats your worldly desire,

Don't deny being a powerful soul you've surpass the bar,

You are a miracle and fabulous thus far.

IF IT'S BROKE

If it's broke you can fix it,

You can because you're a woman and a solider,

If it's outdated restore it,

You can because you're a woman and you have style,

If it's unknown acknowledge it,

You can because you're a woman and you can bring the dark to light,

If it's unsalvageable to others,

You can renew, you can breath life into it and you can shed light on the unknown because you're a woman.

I'M FEELING GOOD TODAY

I'm feeling good today,
Nothing bad is going to come my way,

I'm feeling like a bird soaring above,
Nothing can bring me down but love,

I'm feeling sharp as a tack,
Nothing can come between me and my mind
because I will attack,

I'm feeling you feeling me,
I don't want nobody in my trap it's important
for me to remain free.

I'M THANKFUL

When I woke up this morning I thank God,

When I received passionate pleasures last night
I thanked my man,

When I arrived at work I thank my boss for his
appreciation for my contributions to his
organization,

When I have this awesome hair I thank my
hairdresser,

When I drink, eat, sleep, laugh and cry I thank
God, I thank God, I thank God.

YOU'VE BEEN

You've been acting so differently lately I hardly
recognized the person you are,

Your honesty is so refreshing I hardly believe
you were the same deceitful person I fell hard
for,

You've been regrouping, rethinking, and
reworking a situation that you were meant to
redo,

You've been showing me a part of you that I've
has been missing.

ADDICTION

The road to recovery has took me many places,
Not all of the roads were nice little spaces,

My love for you is crazy,
All I want to do is lie around and be lazy,

I take from people and strangers alike,
I need its comfort to get through the night,

I lie, cheat, and steal,
My body is frail from not having a meal,

My children have to help me,
Because these cravings I have I'm unable to
break free,

When I visit family and friends they hide their
things,
They know I'll take their money and rings,

My parents attend church to pray for my safe
return to them,
What they don't realize it's got a hold on me
like those other hoodlums,

I once was this person, who didn't believe in
getting high,
One weak moment I gave it a try,

Today I'll face another challenge to be release
from its grip,
Or do I take another trip.

A GOOD WOMAN

A good woman will find a good man,
She doesn't have to play games to obtain the
partner of her choice,

A good woman will hold her own,
She does not have to rely on anyone to provide
for her basic needs,

A good woman will make a will and a way,
She has the assets to delegate,

A good woman will not give her all and not
have anything left for her,

A good woman will seize the opportunity,
She'll savior the moment and enjoy her life as it
is.

ALL

All the lies, deceit and cheating nobody cares,

All the wars, killing and murder nobody cares,

All the greed, lust and money everybody cares.

ALWAYS TOLD

They always told me you're so strong,
I was proud so I loaded my shoulders,

They always told me you're so independent,
I was proud so I never asked for help,

They always told me you're so smart,
I was proud so I overachieved,

They always told me you're so beautiful,
I was proud so I emulated others, who I
thought reflected me,

They always told me how proud they are of my
accomplishments,
I was proud, overwhelmed, joyous and
miserable.

AWAKENING

A lazy Sunday morning,
All you want to do is try to lay in bed and
continue yawning,

The sweet aroma of coffee brewing,
Reading the paper not wondering what the
others are doing,

A soft kiss on the cheek,
A pleasant surprise to make your knees weak,

You hear a little voice calling your name,
Loving to cuddle without any shame,

Finding a quite moment to write,
Having to wait until midnight,

All is peaceful and still,
Getting ready to prepare tomorrow's meal,
You cherish the time you couldn't ask for a
better deal,

The next day has come,
New memories have just begun.

BAGGAGE

The time has come for me to address my
concerns,
I feel them coming to the surface from each
lesson learned,

I'm carrying baggage in my head,
It's about time I renewed my thoughts and put
them to bed,

I need to feel alive,
Drop those useless burdens and go for a drive,

My mission is to get myself right,
Stay on a straight path and take that to a new
height,

I cannot be blinded by love or affection,
I have to clear my way first and take it in a
new direction,

Not worrying about my destination,
Releasing the old ways feeling a new sensation,

Getting to know myself is such a pleasure,
My life, my choice and my faith is the treasure.

BAR SCENE

Sometimes driving in the car,
I wonder why on every corner there's a bar,

Are we as a society required to have these
establishments by law?
Every week you hear on the news about some
kind of brawl,

I past several where there's a ladies night,
The next one's a gentleman's club that takes
flight,

Entertainment runs rampant at the sports spot,
They offer the games in high definition which
is really hot,

Rumors go around while drinks are being
watered down,
Conversations get heated until the event
sounds,

There are many varieties of bars to choose from
in the city,
I'd love to see more beautiful buildings and
parks what a pity.

BELIEVE

Believe in your dreams or your hopes will fade,

Believe faith has brought you far and your
goals will become a reality,

Believe you have made the right decisions and
your mind will not wander,

Believe in yourself as God believes in you.

BE STRONG

Be strong my sister things are going to change,
You have the strength, perseverance and
endurance,

Be strong my sister you health depends on it.
You have discipline, tenacity and patience to
change the outcome,

Be strong my sister life is vibrant, a mystery
and plentiful.

Be strong.

BLUE

Some wear blue others black,

They carry a big stick and ready for attack,

I've watched their negative image on TV,

There's a commotion in the street and they
swarm to the scene like a bee,

Uphold the law they are told to do,

I know and you know this is not always true,

We call on the phone in despair,

Oh! Do they really care?

The next time you see those swirling lights,

Pray their resolving a dilemma in their flights.

BROTHER MAN

Brother man Brother Man why are you always faking it,
Brother man Brother Man why are you making me apart of your issues,

Brother man Brother Man why do you put your personal business on Front Street,
Brother man Brother man why are you quick to shut out your Nubian queen,

Brother man Brother Man why do you smoke, drink, and blame others for your dysfunctional self,
Brother man Brother Man why can't you sit back review, rewind and redo your current situation,

Brother man Brother Man why do you run away from love and hold onto negativity,
Brother man Brother Man why can't you hold your women the way you hold your privates,

Brother man Brother Man why do you hold your emotions, your dreams and hopes from us,
Brother man Brother man when you disrespect us you discredit our ancestors, our community and children,

Brother man Brother Man stand up for us stand up for your character, stand up.

CALL GIRL

Growing up she had a full proof plan,
She would marry a wealthy man,

She used her body as a gift,
She occasionally took drugs to give herself a lift,

Her lifestyle was a delight,
She still had many of battles to fight,

She knew in twenty years her beauty would
fade,
She invested the money she made,

She knew her time was near,
She had to give up her living out of fear,

The money she made paid for her meals,
The IRS told her no more deals,

To make matters worst her first client took half,
She would mail him the check in a draft,

What was said of her career?
It was doomed and her assets were in the rear,

She had friends galore,
When her money was gone they all left her for a
new score.

CHANCES

Chances are if you're doing the same thing everyday your not growing or expanding,

Chances are if you make a to do list everyday and nothing gets accomplished is because your not making an effort to cross of what's necessary and keeping what's important,

Chances are if you're still in an unfulfilling relationship you haven't grown and your stuck in the same mind set,

Chances are if your conversation is about the same thing, person or place you need to turn the page and begin a new chapter.

CONCEIT

It's not just me,
Nor will it ever be,

I'm surrounded by selfish folks,
How hypocritical and what a joke,

I sit still in my small cubicle watching waiting
for someone to assist,
I'm feeling uneasy I want to scream by I resist,

I drive home from the mall,
I'm shocked to see   the lack of Samarians
their numbers are small,

I wait in line at the store,
And no one stops to open the door,

I listen to music on the radio in my car,
It shocks me by how these artists think money is
the star,

The story plots I view on TV,
They think its all about me,

Who else in this world thinks free?
And agree I hope it's not just me.

CONFUSED

When she was a little girl it was brutal and
cold,
She had to deal with issues her mind could not
hold,

Her thoughts were confused and dazed,
She was abused and her mind and body in a
haze,

She was unloved and ignored,
She wanted to take her life but most times she
ran for the door,

Her friends were her family and solace,
They never understood her present place,

She would be with who ever loved her at the
time,
They give her more drama and didn't help her
worth a dime,

She prayed she would be free of this hell.
It felt like she was living inside a jail,

She wanted to be rescued from her personal
death wish,
She tried time and time again to recruit many
people off her list,

She was frighten by the things that were done for free,
She was trapped and they wouldn't let her be,

Her mind was sharp as a tack,
If she told anyone she would get a whack,

Her parents were selfish they trusted everyone,
They were blind and could not see what had been done;

She held onto the belief that one day it would be greater,
She didn't know it would come several decades later.

CONSUMPTION

I wanted to run to the store,
I was craving so much more,

I was living for tomorrow and on borrowed
time,
I needed to get those errands done and spend
every extra dime,

It's always a vacation, holiday or birthday
alert,
I will not let those I love go berserk,

I have to supply everyone with everything,
If only I refrain from spending my hard earn
money ching ching.

CUSTOMER SERVICE

Everyone wants things immediately done,
I shiver because I know it'll be awhile and the
craziness has just begun,

Dealing with the changes and procedures of
the everyday event,
I often wonder why I chose this position
because at any moment I'm ready to vent,

I feel unappreciated and a little stiff,
I'm trying to please people and that's no small
gift,

My breaks are short lunch is in a flash,
Trying to get sales for commission because I'm
strapped for cash,

I'm yelled at, disrespected and told it's all my
fault,
I feel like a victim just after an assault,

The praises are far and few between,
Most times people are rude and just plain mean,

The calls come in at a fast rate,
Do I risk taking a personal day for Pete sake?

Fixing problems and taking bill payments all
day,
I run for the door to a much needed get away.

DECEPTION

She's not young and thin,
Society considers her an outcast so they won't
let her in,

The commercials on TV have pills, gadgets and
lotions,
They think they've found a miracle youth
potion,

She doesn't read the daily newspaper it's
loaded with drug dealers, rapist and thieves,
It's horrific entertainment causing us to grieve,

She's full figured, brown skin with a pretty face,
She's the outcast and distant from the human
race,

She reads magazines that exploit the rich by
what they wear, where they live, and who they
date,
She's enraged and full of so much hate,

In the media they may throw in an ounce of
joy,
Where the stocks are, what's the weather, and
who's nominated for a music award,
It's often overshadowed by murder and she gets
bored,

She likes to feed her mind with positive thoughts, faith, uplifting emotions, These thoughts cannot be cured by pills, gadgets and lotions.

DEPRESSION

I know I haven't been myself lately but that's
okay,
Tomorrow will come and I'll be in a better way,

I think of myself as a caring person, who
provides joy,
At times my mood is disturbing Oh! Boy,

I'm not on my monthly or menopause,
Today I just have a dark shadow behind me
and I don't know the cause,

Thinking about the last time I was happy,
I cringe inside because it's been so long ago
and I'm still crappy,

The delusion of someone I once knew,
I wish just for today I didn't feel blue.

DIVA

She shops for clothes, jewelry and shoes,
She loves paying interest and not being picky
on what credit card she choose,

She makes regular trips to the mall,
Spending is her passion and she's having a ball,

Smelling good and having new things all the
time,
She doesn't care about laying down her last
dime,

Traveling to exotic places of her choice,
She's living for today and she frequently likes
to rejoice,

Living paycheck to paycheck and pay day loans,
Her only tragedy is she doesn't have an
audience that moans,

She thinks highly of herself,
She doesn't realize the damage she's doing to
her wealth,

She's content to live this make believe story,
She's blind to the real world and all its true
glory.

DOES IT REALLY MATTER

Does it really matter what other people think
about you in this place,
Your only required to do what you feel is right
and at your own pace,

Does it really matter if you choose to go left
when your family prefers you to go right?
You only did what your spirit compelled you to
do so you could soar to a new height,

Does it really matter that you have not
committed to your soul mate,
You know when to decide on that date,

Does it really matter how long it takes for you
to complete that journey to one,
Your personal discovery is not satisfactory
much work is needed to be done,

Does it really matter to the masses that you are
struggling with your own turmoil?
Your concerns with self is important and your
strengths will not be foiled,

Does it really matter?

EMPOWERMENT

If all goes well with what we seek,
There would be no room for you to feel weak,

If everyday were sunny and bright,
All of god's children would live in delight,

There are so many faces in the crowd,
We have to say what we want and say it loud,

So much to distinguish from what is true,
We must believe in ourselves and know what to
do,

You will get bumps and bruises along the way,
But the journey to peace is not far away,

Your heart maybe heavy from the climb,
 Keep in mind you can wash away the dirt and
grime,

Stay still a moment to receive your good in life,
Feeling the pain is temporary no need to
struggle or strife,

You must maintain your morals,
If not you will continue to have inner turmoil,

Love yourself first,
You're the only one who can quench your thirst.

ESTEEM

She wanted circumstances different in her life,
Shortly after puberty she was an older man's
wife,

Her child had come when she was a teen,
She had no money, education and nothing in
between,

She craved affection, intimacy and love,
Searching underneath a man and sometimes
above,

Her desire to be wanted was fleeing and much
too fast,
It was due to her upbringing and her horrific
past,

Her misconceptions of relationships and caring
for herself first,
Left her wanting any attention to quench her
needy thirst,

At last, she has forgave her polluted mind,
Her wounds have healed and solitude was not
hard for her to   find.

EVERYDAY

Every day is a wonderment of what I discover about you,

Every day is as exciting as the first time we met,

Every day is a lesson learned from the experiences you've showed me,

Every day is filled with happiness I've never expected to feel from anyone,

Every day I thank you God,

Every day is a new beginning to an everlasting love,

Every day I think of the things, the ideas and the promises yet to be fulfilled.

FEEL FREE

If I were a love song I would be a slow Ballard,
I consider myself sweet, soft and a soul
searching person,

If I were a bird I like to be swan,
I'm vulnerable, gentle and easy to capture,

If I were seafood I would be a shrimp,
I enjoy being soaked, peeled and seasoned just
so,

If I were a book I would have to be a thriller,
I'm mysterious, suspenseful and a cliff hanger,

If I were to be anything I would be all things
because being open to different experiences
gives me positive results.

FOOD

It's comforting in a stressful environment,
Morning, noon and midnight it's sheer
contentment,

It's usually overdone when you do not give it
your full attention,
Smelling that awesome aroma could provide a
better prevention,

Sitting at your desk it's all around you,
You grab at anything by the twos,

When company stops by that's the first thing
that cross your mind,
You'll have those pots and flames going in no
time,

With all this preparation the weight picks up a
pound,
You try to cut back but the temptation is all
around,

You say in your mind it's not your friend,
All the while you rank it in your top ten.

FOREVER YOUNG

We are overlooked because our bottom drop,
What's not understood is we use our heads now
to stay on top,

We are seen least attractive to the masses
because our hips are swell,
What's not understood were beautiful to
ourselves so you go to hell?

We are told we need to lose weight and get our
tummies tuck,
What's not understood is we prevail over these
petty issues only the weak will get stuck,

We are more than meets the eye,
What's misunderstood is we are the one's who
uplift you surprise,

We don't try to be nothing we are not,
If you think you don't need us you better stop,

We prefer to be strong in our endeavors,
What's unspoken we can do it better.

FORWARD MARCH

Mind your business and keep it moving,

I love my life because it's grooving,

Me and the Lord have our hands full,

I don't have time to feed into your bull,

Talking behind my back will not help your cause,

I'm on a mission and you're stuck on pause,

Don't worry about me everything's tight,

My worlds in tack and I'll be alright.

GREED

I want it at a discount price,
It doesn't matter what device,

I don't want it later I want it now,
It doesn't matter what the size or if the color is
brown,

I crave the taste of it,
Even if it's a small fit,

I want what you had,
Even if it's just a fad,

Give it to me,
I want it for free,

It may make me fat,
I don't care about that,

It may leave me broke,
I'll laugh it off like a joke,

I won't wait all day,
 I'll ask for it in another way.

GONE

Gone are the unhappy moments,
Gone are the negative thoughts,
Gone are the unhealthy habits.
Gone are the shoulda, woulda ,coulda,
Gone are the tears making room for cheers.

GRIEF

Steam evaporating from the rain,
I want to relieve my pain,

He's been gone for eight long years,
Today I remember him vividly and I'm trying
to hold back my tears,

I recall our last conversation me telling him to
explain,
My mind wonders and I become drain,

We went to the movies and to the mall,
Oh! We had a ball,

We laughed and joked for awhile,
It was like when he was a child,

We sat in silence on the ride home,
I felt emptiness and soon I would be alone,

I wish today I could relive the fun,
Today I feel sorrow because I miss my only son.

HOW DEEP

A wish fulfilled,
Feeling grateful for life's little pleasures,
What are the topics the general population
craves?
Thinking of a summer love and the comfort it
bought you,
Remember someone who had an addiction to
drugs and loved the escape of it,
Grieving over a loved one,
Involved with someone who wanted access to
your things and not your pain,
Watching music videos and wondering if
you're a contender,
Holding on to that Miss Independent role,
Trying to recall love and all it's splendor,
Not living enough for today,
Pushing yourself too the limit,
Praising your accomplishments and your
ability,
Taking little advice from friends and family,
Putting to much in a relationship,
Having positive reactions and interactions,
Feeling outrage by watching the disturbing
events of the day,
Keep New Year's resolutions,
Listening to girlfriends with an open mind,
Commitment to change,
Strong ties to family,
Staying on your own terms,
Leaving bad situations,

Having goals,
Being determine of the reality of the goals,
Loving feelings towards yourself and others,
Viewing the brightside of the positive and
negative,
Human abilities and seeing them push forward.

IMAGINATION

I want to cry but I don't want to feel sorry for myself,

I want to dance but my rhythm is a little off,

I want to shout to the world I'm happy but the world with all its extremes would not accept this fate.

I'M TOO MUCH FOR YOU

I'm too much for you,
I run a household, I hold down a career and I
make my own money,

I'm too much for you,
I can produce food for an infant, I can get free
drinks on ladies night and I can get assistance
from my girlfriends,

I'm too much for you,
I cook, I clean and I can make you shiver,

I'm too much for you,
I can achieve and believe because I'm too
much for you.

I WANT

I want to walk on the wild side,

I want to speak several different languages,

I want one day a week where I'm catered to,

I want a picnic poolside on top of a glass
building,

I want to receive just as much as I give,

I want to pray for the elderly and sick,

I want God to forgive me for not putting her
first in all the things I want.

KINDNESS

I take a second to say thank you,
It's effortlessly to smile at someone,
You may feel down but what you do for others
will bring you joy with open arms.

LAY IT DOWN

Some situations have you in a scare,
You think you're the only one and nobody
cares,

Rethinking your journey in one fall swoop,
Putting out small fires and still you remain in
the same loop,

 Not to long ago life was sweet,
 Today your back's against the wall and your
feeling defeat,

Keeping the demons at bay,
Trying to focus in your own way,

Your body's in withdrawal like being hooked
on dope,
The mind stays strong and you pray you can
cope,

Today the sun is shining you won the fight,
God placed his hands on you to make your
burdens light,

One day you'll meet her at the pearly gate,
No more fears to negotiate.

LEARNING

With the detriment of paper and book,
Our school policies require a fresh look,

Change starts at home for students to learn,
That approach helps the teachers give them
moments to yearn,

Teachers are not being praised for a job well
done,
Getting unwanted publicity from a pupil
bringing in a gun,

Music and art are being removed at a rapid
rate,
Because of the lack of funding from the state,

Not much emphasis on special education,
We need qualified individuals for enhanced
edification,

If the fiscal budget can fit legal gambling into
play,
Our institutions of learning should expand the
same way.

MAY I SUGGEST

You are all over the place,
May I suggest you find your space?

You take more you give some,
May I suggest you sit still instead of being on
the run?

You love the spotlight,
May I suggest you get right?

You're a spiritual being,
May I suggest you start seeing?

You've found love, you've lost love,
May I suggest you speak with the man above?

You do for others in their time of need,
May I say that's fine indeed?

ME

Everyone's pushing their responsibly on each
other,
Gone are the days were looking out for one
another,

It's all about me not you,
You don't have a clue,

I got mine,
It's all fine,

I love this game,
I'll always remain the same,

I'm laughing behind your back,
I know where to attack,

I'll show sorrow in your face,
You'll know soon about my disgrace,

I'll move on to the next one,
This is sure lots of fun.

NO DOUBTS

I'm disappointed with women today,
There acting so desperate in every way,

What's up with women checking their man's
cell phones, pants pockets, and personal stuff?
I want you to love yourself enough,

Get to know that male inside and out,
Therefore, you'll be sure and don't have a
doubt,

Don't panic if things aren't going well,
You did your best so what the hell,

The next time you feel despair,
Think before you overreact and share,

I know you want to love someone,
Take it slow with them before they run,

You must respect yourself not belittle one
another,
Maybe one day you can trust that brother.

ONCE

I once thought misery loves company,
I once thought dreams never become a reality,
I once thought love for oneself was far fetched,
I once thought you only needed one soul mate,
I once thought anger gave you the power,
I once thought I only could go as far as the
glass ceiling,
Look at me now; I'm not caught up in those
thoughts.

NOBODY ASK ME TO DANCE ANYMORE

Nobody asks me to dance anymore,
My youthful days partying I had more men
than I could count with both hands,

Nobody asks me to dance anymore,
My agile moves have become a slow grind,

Nobody asks me to dance anymore,
I no longer succumb to the over made up face
or provocative clothes,
Is it because nobody asks me to dance anymore.

OUR WORLD

The recommendation that I'm about to make
will cause a major uproar,
I've been compelled to talk about this issue and
much more,

I want everyone to be well and in good health,
It requires taking care of your inner self,

Babies are required to receive our love and
care,
These major components are a pair,

Our elders are wise and have seen things our
generation has only read about,
I dear not question them, disapprove or show
doubt,

We all should try to be responsible for ourselves,
our families and our world,
Opening our hearts to the concerning perils.

PERSONAL JOURNEY

Why should I blame me?
I don't control the powers that be,

I'm unable to sit around and complain all day,
Waiting for my goodness to display,

The choices I've made paved my fate this day,
this month and this year,
I've put on my game face and did a personal
cheer,

I've always looked up to someone else's glory,
I've restored my esteem now I'm ready to tell
my own story,

I was on this insane ride,
Now I have to do or die,

I carry my own burdens heavy or light,
I know in the end I'm going to be alright.

PERSONALITIES

I have a friend, who always calls for a favor or two,
I make up excuses because if I need her help she won't do,

I have a friend, who has a problem with men,
She makes excuses for them every now and then,

I have a friend, who's always buying stuff,
She has a problem of never having enough,

I have a friend, who knows it all,
I don't entertain her much I rarely take her call,

I have a friend, who doesn't complain,
She's meek and has room for confidence to gain,

I have a friend, who's pretty on the outside unsure within,
She thinks if only she had love in her life everything would not seem so grim.

POSSIBILITES

Take one step at a time,
Dare to go beyond these dark thoughts,
Soar in your mind to a place where you are
truly happy,
Make those dreams possible,
Open your eyes it's all coming true.

POWER

It takes two elements to decide,

It's one on one and side by side,

It takes a group to motivate,

It's takes you its takes me to cultivate,

It takes many to bring about change,

It's you, me the world were all within range.

REALITY

Love gone bad love is good,
Money short living in the hood,

Black is in,
But was it out I have to rethink that again,

Days are gloomy nights are poppin,
The oldies radio station is non stopping,

Feeling the winter blast on your face,
Summer's six months away the season for lace,

Prices on goods going up and down,
Trying to find a reasonable mortgage on the
other side of town,

Laying on your morals is crazy,
The world is in a crisis all around us there's no
time to be lazy.

RESTRUCTURE

The time has come to rise above your current
place,
Evacuate those old problems that's been sitting
dormant taking up space,

The time has arrive for you to embrace your
present self with love,
Being grateful for the heaven above,

The time has expired to feel negative about
things beyond your control,
Taking strength in your solace and becoming
bold,

The time has come to put your life, your
household and your money on the line,
Improving these qualities will assure your
prospects will run just fine.

ROLE MODEL

I'm the woman with the most,
I have to glide through life not coast,
Every now and then I'll brag or boast,

I have to represent big time,
The bridges I build now will be my shrine,
I will be so fierce they'll call it a crime,

I will create a path of positive moves for all to
adore,
My goal is to uplift and provide more,
Being true to myself and helping others for sure,

I have to motivate and show the real me,
So much work ahead I can't let others be,
My show to the world is not free,

I'm doing this for love not money,
I have sheer determination honey,
My views are way to cutting,

Hard work for me is not just a fling,
I do it to reach the masses not for the brass
ring,
This is not Hollywood no glitter or bling,

I will take the good along with the bad,
My methods may make others mad,
This journey is not just a fade,

I'm here to teach and mold,
I'll be doing this until I'm old,
I will uplift my followers to shine and be bold.

ROTTEN

You've been sheltered all through out your
childhood,
You were pampered like a princess and up to no
good,

You attended the best school, had the best
teachers and had the best class,
You got distracted by some peers, whose
behavior was trash,

You were loved and cherished,
It seems nowadays all of your hopes and
dreams have perished,

You walk around your parent's home and tell
them you're grown,
As soon as you have a problem you're calling
them on the phone,

They don't want to abandon you to the streets,
Many have come and gone under from its
defeat,

They'll love you more than anyone out there,
They don't want you to be harmed or feel
despair,

They had to let go,
Let you orchestrate your own show,

Their position now is in the background,
May you discover your path and remember
faith can easily be found.

RUSH

Hit the snooze several times,
Roll out of bed,
Take a quick shower,
Wake the children and husband,
Find an outfit for work,
Grab you coat and keys,
Get in your car,
Child needs a ride,
Car tank on empty,
Gonna be late for work,
Drop child off at the bus stop,
Pull up to gas the station,
Attendant tallying his draw,
Try to use several credit cards none work,
Dig up cash in the glove box,
Arrive late for work,
Your turn to lead the meeting,
Picked up child's report by mistake,
Memorized key topics,
Get to your desk,
Check emails,
Return some calls,
Forgot your lunch again,
Coworker shares hers,
Go back to your desk,
Note on desk from boss wants you in her office,
On probation for excessive lateness,
Return to desk makes several more calls,
Check on personal business from this morning,
End of the day is here,

Rush out the building,
Car tie flat,
Wait for tow truck,
Two hours pass,
To do list done,
Off to the market to pick up dinner,
Arrive home to a mess,
Dinner prepared and cooked,
Homework finished,
Catch a sitcom,
Exhausted from today's events,
Preparing for tomorrow's rush.

SAME GENDER

You like someone the same as you are,
Because society says it's not right you adore
them from afar,

You're afraid to admit how deep you feel,
If you tell anyone they may become ill,

You want to come out and tell the world,
That you involved and love that girl,

Your parent's standards are outdated and old,
You tell them about this delicate secret you had
on hold,

Their upset about your choice,
You want them to be happy and rejoice,

They feel they didn't do their best,
Looking at your personal life as if it's a mess,

You're trying to accept what you told them in
love,
One parent tells you that you'll suffer from the
man above,

You put yourself in their shoes,
Just waiting it out your patience is due.

SECRET

Let me tell you a secret,
I want you to hold this within,

Because the complexity of its contents I will
bestow on you for a very long time,
I know you value our friendship and would not
betray me,

That would be a sin to share and divulge
something so sacred,
This proves to me that you are loyal,

I on the other hand am free of this burden,
guilt, and shame thanks.

SELF

I have a friend I'll call her Awesome,
She's frugal, funny and knows what battles she
can win,

I have a friend I'll call her Lovely,
She's a fashion icon, well traveled and knows
what food to order when fine dining,

I have a friend I'll call her Marvelous,
She's spiritual, well preserved and can smooth
your wounded heart,

I have a friend I'll call her Cookie,
She's awesome, lovely and totally marvelous.

SOAR

I'm not a party girl you won't catch me at the
club,
I'm the type, who likes long baths in the tub,

I love to read a human interest story,
I'm not into the ones about fame and glory,

I savior life and all that it gives,
It will benefit me as long as I live,

I'm always asked if I'll walk that extra mile,
I reply yeah with a great big smile,

I always keep my future in sight,
My imagination soars and takes me to a new
height,

Sometimes in my journeys I may get hurt,
I brush off those feelings and firmly plant my
feet in the dirt,

Doing what I do is not a trick,
I like to stay focus uninvolved with a click,

At times an issue may have me stuck,
 I pray I get through it with a little luck,

Some may consider me a snob,
That's there problem I'm doing a job,

What I continue to do brings me joy,
I'm sincere and slightly coy,

I don't want to show bravado or dwell,
Through all my work things are going well.

STEP UP

Step up and out of your own way,
Are you intelligent?
If not, it's time to start today,

Step up to your purpose in this new light,
You've overcome many obstacles this one's a
small plight,

Step up your game,
Stop being so lame,

Step up to the plate,
You're not too late,

Step up be relentless and strong,
The passage you take is not going to be wrong,

Step up to your greatness and be heard,
You need this experience don't just take my
word.

SURREAL

I detest women being exploited by the masses,
I pray for one moment in time I could address
this to all races, creed and classes,

We are intelligent, beautiful and we bring the
thunder,
It's a surreal wonder,

How is she still able to do this?
We stay focus unlike others with their hit or
miss,

You're more interested in our body than our
brain,
Your so obsess with our fixtures it's insane,

Making money off our assets is an option for
you,
We use our mind, talents and abilities this is
true,

Don't keep disrespecting your ultimate queen,
She's your partner and deserves to be heard
and seen.

THANK GOD

May I cry on your shoulder for awhile?
God you're my savior and I'm your child,

May I ask that you forgive my sin?
I will pray more often tell me where to begin,

May I wash my hands in your holiness?
With you in my life I will overcome all
loneliness,

May my cup run over in your good grace?
I know with you in my heart I have no need to
save face,

May you always make me aware of you?
My life is full because of your blessings that you
thought I was due,

May I take heed and know the devil is a liar
this time,
Oh! Lord with you by my side it's not a crime.

THE FIRST TIME

I didn't know what to expect from the caress or touch,
I was scared and he was in such a rush,

Holding my hand and roughly lowering me down,
Kissing me stiffly I had to frown,

I became distraught by his lack of skill,
In a minute my stomach felted ill,

Everything was over and done,
No hugs or thank you just a quick shun,

My adventure was not a fairytale story,
It was pitiful without all the glory.

THE GIG

If you're late they reduce your pay,
It's a child care emergency today,

Sometimes it's unavoidable to make a mistake,
The policies are always changing its no longer
a piece of cake,

All day long you receive the same call,
You need an unscheduled break to go to the
mall,

You come in early for a meeting to get the full
detail,
However, you're delayed because the hello's
had you derailed,

No appreciation and no perk for a job well
done,
Only for a few chosen ones son of gun,

All year long you look forward to the Christmas
party they plan,
Just to find out here's your last check so long
man.

THE OBITUARY

Love is the beginning,
Death is the end and in between there's birth.

THE PRESENT

I have witnessed a steady stream of events,
My mind is still strong the memories have no
dents,

My president is black,
He's doesn't take no flack,

Women are the new bread winners,
They are no longer the beginners,

The youth are wise beyond their years,
Making the elders sit back feeling joy with
much cheers,

Were in a recession,
This contributes to our overwhelming
depression,

Our history is unfolding at alarming rates,
By the time this goes to print, we'll have more
history making greats.

TODAY

Today is the best day of my life,

I didn't curse anyone out,

Today is the day I feel joy,

I smiled and told myself to start a new chapter,

Today I'll forgive others for feeling inadequate about themselves,

I feel love in my heart and I will spread it all around,

Yesterday was a blessing,

Tomorrow will be the same.

UNTITLED

I have many stories to tell,
They were a burden that made my thoughts
swell,

Releasing the context from my mind,
Put me in a better place to unwind,

At times I'd be angry and couldn't understand,
How could I feel better with just a pen in my
hand?

I was contemplating writing a book,
There were many topics I had to take a second
look,

Should I consider a love story?
Too many in circulation I might as well do a
science fiction that's gory,

I'm leaning towards a suspense thriller,
Maybe about a cold blooded killer,

Looking over my bookshelf there's a selective
mix,
I should start soon to find that perfect fix.

VACATION

It's that time of the year,
We have our gadgets and our gear,

We're required each year to get some sun,
I want to get to the beach I need a little fun,

I budget and save for several months or so,
My expectations are high my funds low,

I enjoy no cell, no TV no laptop,
I'm sipping on some exotic drink nonstop,

My week has past,
I've had a blast,

Back to work the next day,
That's what they think because I'll come up
with an excuse to get my way,

I love time to be carefree,
Is taking off an extra day too much for the
powers that be?

WASTED TIME

Sitting in the front of the television,
Not preparing that resume' revision,

Talking on the phone,
Instead of enjoying sometime alone,

Shopping at the mall,
Instead of learning to sew using a pattern by
McCall,

Gossiping about a movie star,
This will not take you far,

Looking good on the outside,
Improving within will show pride,

Sipping on a drink is not cool after awhile,
We can show our children this before they
become wild,

The computer has lots of helpful information,
But a hands on approach provides a better
situation,

Having unprotected sex is a foolish choice,
Cherish your body it's your temple rejoice,

Being selfish is not divine,
Sharing with friends improves your life and
extends your joyous times.

WHO ARE YOU

What you think you know about a person today
can surely change by tomorrow,

You talk to this person hours on end and you
know for sure your intuition has not failed you,

What you are experiencing is a change in the
situation not the person,

They may have been this way all along,

However, you were just tuned into the physical
being,

One day soon you look at this person with
empty eyes,

Your admiration has filtered a bit but it's just
as strong as it was the day you started loving
them,

You try to make sense of your feelings,

Your mind goes blank because you want to
retain the memory of the person you didn't
know.

WHO'S THE MOST HATED

Who's hated the cop?
He acts like he's on top,
And just about to get pop,

Who's hated the paper?
Humans running around like a midnight
caper,
Wanting to look tailored and tapered,

Who's hated the opposite of the man?
She's sure of herself and knows she can,
Knowing the possibly and sizzling like a steak
in a hot frying pan.

WHY AM I

Why am I always the one that's touched not held?

Why am I always the one, who's looked at not seen?

Why am I always the one falling in love and not loved?

Why I am always the one being pushed not praised,

Why am I always the one to see it and not have it?

YOU LIED

You lied to me when you told me my body was heaven sent,

You lied to me when you said you'd never leave me,

You lied to me when you said you would never disrespect me,

You lied to me when you told me you wanted to marry me because you were in a desperate space,

You lied to me when you said I was your angel your rock,

You lied to me when you said you would attend church services with me,

You lied to me from the beginning, the middle and the end.

YOU'RE RESPONSIBLE

Women are the queens of their castles,
Our men are suppose to take care of us without
any hassles,

We are there to be your caretakers,
Not just your baby makers,

No problem should arise when we request
something,
When we took our vows and signified it with a
ring,

You're responsible for the home,
Were not required to go it alone,

The next time I hear a men complain about his
other half,
I'll direct him on the right path.

YOURS TRULY

You will have trouble entering in your next relationship because of the profound way I treated you heart,

You won't reach that plateau because you didn't hold my heart the way I held yours.

Breinigsville, PA USA
13 May 2010
237930BV00001B/25/P